AF885479

Tax Risk in the 21st Century

How to Manage Tax Risk like a Big Company Without the Big Expense

Ana Sainz

Tax Risk in the 21st Century

Published by:
90-Minute Books
302 Martinique Drive
Winter Haven, FL 33884
www.90minutebooks.com

Published in the United States of America

ISBN-13: 978-0692520451
ISBN-10: 0692520457

For more information on 90-Minute Books including finding out how you can publish your own lead generating book, visit www.90minutebooks.com or call (863) 318-0464

Here's What's Inside…

Toronto, Canada
November 2015

Companies need to effectively manage tax risk. The push for improvement in the tax risk area began in the early 2000s when a few well-known corporations manipulated tax figures which contributed to their demise. Companies are increasingly becoming aware of the risk exposure lying within tax departments and the need to develop policies, procedures, and mandates to address the risk.

Having a corporate level risk management strategy in place is the norm and tax risk should be a component of that strategy but companies are a little anxious when it comes to addressing tax. It might be you don't see tax as a risk, which is a risk in itself if you think about it, or it's the very large price tag that generally comes with this kind of specialized work (or maybe both).

What follows are the basic strategies we use at The Claret Partners Limited to help clients manage tax risk and create tax risk strategies at a reasonable price. Managing tax risk like a Big Company doesn't have to come with a big price tag.

Enjoy the Book!

We hope this book educates and encourages you to manage your tax risk.

To Your Success!

Ana Sainz & The Claret Partners Limited

Why Tax Risk Management Is More Critical than Ever

Historically, tax was, in large part looked upon as something to avoid; dealt with for as little time as possible and generally not well resourced. Then the world shrank, corporations began operating in many different tax jurisdictions and became myopically focused on share price. Creative tax advisors stepped in to assist clients in minimizing taxes and in some cases creating tax profit centres. The lack of knowledgeable oversight by Board members and senior management lead to disastrous results.

In the early 2000s the world stopped to consider the collapse of several global corporations and watch the ripple effect it had on the economy and people's lives. Tax risk was a significant factor in these collapses. Regulators reacted by installing oversight legislation: the Multilateral Instrument 52-110 in Canada, and the US Sarbanes-Oxley ("SOX") Act. The SOX Act created the Public Company Accounting Oversight Board; the impact of which was to subject public company auditors to external oversight from the US Securities Exchange rather than the self-regulation they had been accustomed to previously. The OECD with its significant clout was, and continues, to influence taxing authorities and regulators though its research and papers on tax risk.

The tax world has continued to change since then: many tax authorities have information sharing agreements in place, policy makers across the globe seek to protect their tax base and are busy crafting legislation meant to increase compliance and enforcement capability. Shareholders and analysts are now demanding more transparency through better tax disclosure. This means more audits and a greater demand for consistent documentation and disclosure.

What has not changed sufficiently is how corporations respond. What may have been adequate ten years ago doesn't cut it anymore. An improved approach to responding to tax risk can reduce the monetary impact of penalties and interest and as importantly reduce the threat of reputational damage. This is where this book and suggested tools can help; we will help you identify, document, assess, and manage your embedded tax risk in four areas – compliance, accounting, governance and resources.

Why Don't More Companies Manage Their Tax Risk?

Most companies don't manage their tax risk effectively because tax departments tend to be under resourced. As a result, they may have to go outside to get work done; usually to a Big Four firm with a very expensive price tag. If there is little or no budget it may mean the risk goes unmanaged as the company doesn't believe they can do it themselves.

What we've found in working with clients to manage their tax risk is with the right processes and tool kits in place, a company can manage its tax risk in house and this makes it more attractive for senior management to get on board. In fact, we think companies should do the tax risk work in house; they understand the business the best. Companies may be missing the broader framework and the individual tools needed in order to minimize the workload of such a project but that is what we will share with you today.

Why Do You Need to Manage Tax Risk?

At a bare minimum a company needs to have internal controls over the tax function and file all required returns. This permits sign off of the CFO certification, makes your financial statement auditors happy and keeps the taxing authorities temporarily away.

The better reasons are that managing tax risk needs to be a component of the overall Enterprise Risk Management program used by senior management and the Board to assess opportunities for shareholder growth. Other significant benefits include:

- enhancing communication between tax and other departments,
- streamlining tax processes to improve quality and/or reduce time required to complete,
- addressing internal resources (number and experience) and external resources (budget and use) and
- saving money on penalties and interest.

There are no right or wrong "risks" but the company needs to make conscious decisions; does it increase, decrease, or maintain the amount of risk and does that match with the company's growth plans. By including all potential tax impacts into possible opportunities, better decisions are made and can improve overall capital deployment.

You Might Even Lower Your Risk-Ranking

The federal taxing authority in Canada, the Canada Revenue Agency (the “CRA”), has instituted a risk-based audit cycle, which means they determine how often they visit you by assigning a risk ranking. We prefer less rather than more visits from the tax auditors.

The CRA recently commented its current risk-based audit approach is in line with the OECD’s five pillars of the co-operative compliance – being commercial awareness, impartiality, and proportionality, openness through disclosure and transparency and responsiveness. Since its initial introduction, the CRA has continued to refine its approach with two significant adaptations. The first being companies are now ranked relative to others by industry and regions and the second is the inclusion of behaviourial and industry inherent risk factors into the ranking process. To get a better handle of these factors the CRA has been visiting with senior management to discuss questions dealing primarily with tax risk and its management. Take a look at the CRA questions/risk ranking information request below. How much of this could you currently provide them with?

1. Describe your tax department – number of staff and each person's function.
2. Describe the formalized tax risk management strategy for identifying, assessing, managing, reporting and mitigating risk in operations including names of staff who oversee each step.
3. Do you routinely conduct a review of the corporate tax risk?
4. Provide supporting information to show how senior management and directors are involved in tax matters.
5. Provide a list and function of any tax service providers used.
6. How do you manage non-compliance and what is done when non-compliance is discovered?
7. How do you ensure information used for tax purposes is accurate?
8. How often have you used external auditors for tax services and what is the fee arrangement (contingency)?
9. Provide details of how the tax strategy is consistent with the overall business strategy.
10. Please provide minutes to the risk management committee if the company has one.
11. What are the company's biggest priorities in the tax area?

We have one client who started off with a high-risk ranking due to its industry and would have a relatively short audit rotation. They developed tax risk strategies which weren't a 200-page unwieldy tome but rather a handful of well-written pages as to how they address tax risk and how they have controls and procedures in place to mitigate the tax risk, as well as the company's philosophy toward tax risk. The subsequent audit proved they could walk the walk as well as talk the talk. The documentation and processes fully supported the tax risk strategy statement and as a result they were moved from a high-risk rotation to a low-risk ranking. This means considerably less time spent dealing with taxing authorities and the annoyance of having them in your office.

Remember that doing "nothing" about tax risk is also a decision that has consequences.

What Is an Enterprise Risk Management (ERM) Program?

We mentioned earlier that tax risk should be a component of a company's overall ERM which then begs the question what is an ERM? Enterprise risk at its basic level is the amount of uncertainty a company takes on as it facilitates shareholder growth.

An ERM program has a number of parts described briefly below:

1. Company strategic plan. A company can determine its tolerance for specific levels of risk (the risk appetite) by analysing each of the opportunities outlined in the strategic plan and identifying the associated risk.

2. Risk management policies and procedures. These documents are needed to keep the risks identified in the strategic plan in line with the risk appetite by those assigned with oversight of the risk (typically senior management).
3. Processes implemented to monitor the actual risk against the policies and procedures established and to correct and communicate any deviations.

As the company executes its strategic plan, opportunities may be modified as well as the level of risk; an ERM program is therefore not static and must be periodically evaluated itself to ensure it is capturing the company's relevant risks. Again there are many ongoing parts to the evaluation process:

- Identify and assess the risks associated with the opportunities, and
- Monitor, report, and manage the risks that are identified in respect of those opportunities.

Just because an organization is good at identifying and assessing risk does not mean it has all the tools on hand to effectively monitor, report, and manage the risks.

The Role of the Board in Managing Risk

- The company's Board of Directors is responsible for overseeing the development of an ERM program and generally delegates primary responsibility for the ongoing oversight to one or more of its audit, risk or governance committees. The Board or its committee's ongoing commitment to an ERM programme is generally as follows:
- The Board approves the risk policies to ensure the communication of the risk appetite is articulated correctly to the rest of the company.
- The Board ensures management's mandate and job description describes the risk levels being delegated by the Board to management.
- The Board should ensure the company has a Code of Conduct signed by all employees.
- The Board should receive regular reporting on the status of the risks being managed. Tax operational risk is typically addressed through CFO certification on internal controls over financial statements and recommendations from external auditors, both of which are typically dealt with by the audit committee. This is however only part of the picture for tax and the Board or the committee should receive a tax report communicating all relevant information at least annually.

The Roles of Senior Management in Managing Risk

Senior management plays a leading role in an ERM program and must ensure the Board's risk appetite and policies have been adhered to. Senior management is in charge of implementing policies and procedures that identify, assess, monitor, manage, and correct a risk in their own specific areas. Senior management is responsible for reporting to the Board on the efficacy of the risk appetite relative to the implementation of the strategic plan - any disconnect must be addressed.

Senior management sets the tone and standard for adhering to the risk it has been delegated by the Board; it sets the tax function's objectives. These may be to minimise effective tax rates, reduce cash taxes, find opportunities offshore, lobby on behalf of industry for a particular tax concession, avoid all possible things that would (if publicly known) embarrass the company, etc. In addition, tax needs to look internally and contain/reduce operational risk within the tax function and across functional areas (ie. how do decisions made in other departments impact tax and vice versa?).

Management is responsible for implementing policies and procedures that are the core of the ERM. This means establishing a framework for the tax function in which risk decisions can be executed. The framework needs to be workable – simple enough to be understood but with sufficient parameters to offer concrete support in the decision making process. The framework needs to contain:

- an estimate of the probability of each current and future risk,
- the range (spread) of the probability occurring and
- the dollar impact associated with each range.

Then layer on a requirement to always evaluate the more esoteric factor of reputational risk.

Getting from Point A to Point B

How do we get from corporate level risk to a tax risk?

We start by looking at the company's principle risks. A principle risk is an uncertainty that alone or combined with interrelated risks would impact the corporation negatively **absent existing mitigating controls**.

We then evaluate how tax impacts these principle risks. For an example let's use the example of a retailer with its long list of principle risks as identified from its strategic plan:

- Business continuity,
- Consumer lending practices,
- Financial markets as a source of capital,
- Financial reporting, and
- The ability to execute the growth plan.

So where is the tax risk? Tax risk is obviously in the financial reporting but also in the execution of the corporate strategy as tax is going to be embedded in new product development, off shore purchasing and sales, geographic expansion, acquisitions and divestitures, and many more areas.

Each principle risk can therefore be broken into segments such as operational, financial, and reputational risks which can further be segmented into routine and non-routine risks. Routine risk is an uncertainty that arises due to normal or routine processes – in tax this would be filing the monthly HST returns. Non-routine risks arise when the event does not occur often such as addressing the HST issues related to acquiring another business or company.

So let's drill down from the principle risk to a tax risk to see how they are linked using an exaggerated example:

ABC Company is expanding into Country B and is going to support the expansion by issuing Euro denominated debt. If the debt cannot be raised, the expansion will not proceed or will need to be scaled back.

1. The principle risk is the inability to execute its expansion strategy.
    - Not executing will impact the shareholders' growth and value in the company (real or perceived),
    - The Board may lose faith in managements' abilities.
2. There are operational, financial and reputational risks to not executing the plan.
    - Supply logistics may be frustrated without the expansion.

- Revenue may not hit target expectations and cash flow restricted.
- Equity analysts may downgrade stock if they don't believe management can grow company.
- The embedded tax risk running through the contemplated financing structure may be challenged by domestic or foreign tax authorities. And if the structure needs to be changed it will affect the financing cost and the potential viability of the expansion.

3. Finally, the risk would be non-routine assuming global expansions are not common place for ABC.

Creating the Tax Risk Framework

Let's continue with the scenario from above and use it to illustrate how we build the framework. The tax risk is related to proposed changes to tax law that might make certain cross border lending structures inefficient.

- The probability of the tax law going through is high,
- The impact would be moderate (it would make the debt less cost efficient but still desirable), and
- It would be moving quite quickly towards you; there's a short lead-time.

We have seen different visuals used to represent tax risk over the years; cones, boxes, webs, 3-D surfaces. We tend to stick to the colour coded matrix for two good reasons; it's simple to understand and we don't draw well.

Step 1: Create a mathematical matrix where we assign a probability to the event occurring. We stick to high, medium, low and colour code these red/yellow/green (or whatever floats your boat).

Step 2: Establish the monetary impact of each probability occurring as a percentage, for example 25%, 50%, 75%, or 100%.

Step 3: Assign a function and person who is responsible for addressing the risk, when they need to escalate and to whom.

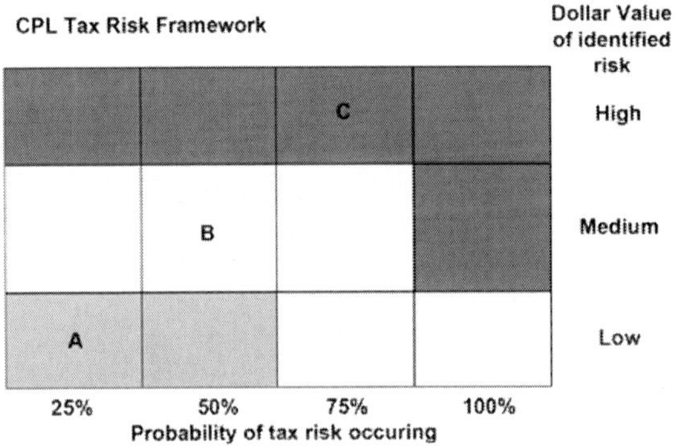

In the visual we see an identified tax risk that falls in the lower bottom zone has a low a dollar value and low probability of occurring.

Tax Risk Thresholds:

Tax Risk Thresholds:

Income taxes only: Canada & USA	Income taxes only: Asia & Europe		Value Added Taxes (VAT) only: Canada	Value Added Taxes (VAT) only: Europe
> 80 million	> 38 million		> 7 million	> 5 million
> 30-80 < million	> 22-38< million		> 1 - 7 < million	> 1.75-5 < million
<30 million	< 22 million		<1 million	<1.75 million

As an example this might mean that in order to be a "green box risk", a specific Canadian income tax risk identified has an expected value of less than C$30 million if it should actually occur and less than a 50% chance of actually occurring. In Asia or Europe the threshold in this example is lower at C$22 million equivalent and VAT related risk amounts are again different. This permits a company to define its various tax jurisdictions with separate thresholds conforming to the company's risk appetite.

The "A", "B" and "C" in the framework should correspond to a title and name responsible for managing the risk and any escalation processes. Consider the following when deciding:

- Who has the authority and the decision-making power for each particular event that falls in the framework?
- If the tax law changes and there is going to be impact on a particular structure, who is responsible for addressing and getting sign off?

- If it is particularly high dollar with high impact coming quickly, does it need to be raised to the board?

Let's tie the example to the framework:

- the known financial impact from switching financing methods is C$72 million over life of debt,
- we believe the probability of the tax law change is 45%,

This is a midrange coded identified risk and person/title B is responsible for decision/resolution and escalation. Board escalation would occur if the dollar value exceeded C$80 million in all cases using the illustrative framework above.

You can see now why it is best that a company tackle these themselves -sit down and assess its risk and decide on how it wants to present them. The matrix will look very different depending on each company's size and risks. The matrix flows to the responsibility and roles and must be fairly detailed; the person in Belgium with a particular tax responsibility may have authority to deal with certain issues in Belgium but may need acknowledgement from the parent office to rectify a larger dollar or regional (all Europe) issue.

Along with the framework visual, policies and procedures must be established and approved by the appropriate level within the company. After the framework is complete, processes for monitoring, mitigating and reporting can begin.

How to Ensure All of Your Tax Risk Is Captured

If identifying risks doesn't come easily you might want to use the decision tree below.

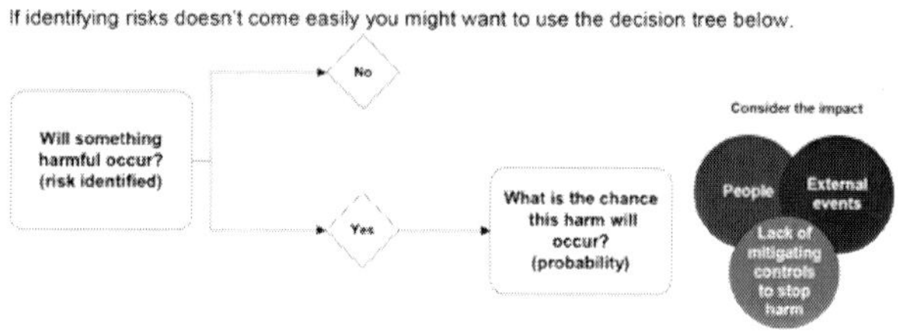

Tax risk generally surfaces as a result of a few or combination of these broad reaching factors:

- Application or interpretation of tax laws,
- Lack of completeness in underlying facts,
- Accounting information is incomplete (insufficient or inaccurate),
- Inexperience or insufficient staffing for workload

We go about ensuring tax risks are captured using our CPL Tax Compass. That CPL Tax Compass is a way to understand the potential risk components. We take you through four main areas of risk, which are governance, compliance, financial accounting, and people and resources. More on that later......

Controlling the Tax Risk

Once a company has its tax risks identified, mitigating procedures need to be implemented and documented. In order to do so, there has to be a core understanding of basic internal control objectives and the related mitigating procedures.

The control objectives are what you want to happen. As an example, if you want your tax expense figures to be timely (objective) then the mitigating procedure would be to ensure that accounting has entered all its transactions into the general ledger and been reviewed before the tax department starts the provision.

Once you have a handle on the control objectives, mitigating procedures with individual key controls can be implemented.

Control Objective	Related Mitigating Procedures						
	Segregation of duties	Pre-numbered documents that are accounted for	Regular reconciliation with independent review	Procedures for prompt recording of transactions	Internal review and verification	Specific and general authorization required at certain points in processing	Chart of Accounts
Validity	✓	✓	✓				
Completeness	✓	✓	✓				
Timeliness				✓	✓		
Authorization						✓	
Measurement					✓		
Classification					✓		✓
Posting and summaries	✓		✓		✓		

An internal control is easiest explained as "the checks and balances" process. There are three types of controls:

1. The preventative control – it catches issues before it makes a mess,
2. The detective control – it finds the mess after the fact and measures the efficacy of preventive controls,

3. The corrective control – it corrects the mess so it doesn't happen again,

Obviously the best (and typically most expensive to employ) are preventative controls. When designing a mitigating control thought has to be given to how effective the control will be and the cost of having the control in place. In addition, you need to consider the impact of the control and whether there are limits to what that control can do once put in place.

We have used the term "key control". A mitigating procedure may have a number of checks and balances (individual controls) but there are usually only a few key controls. Key controls are the ones that matter – as an example, in preparing a tax return there are lots of checks and balances already built into the software but the key control is the detailed review.

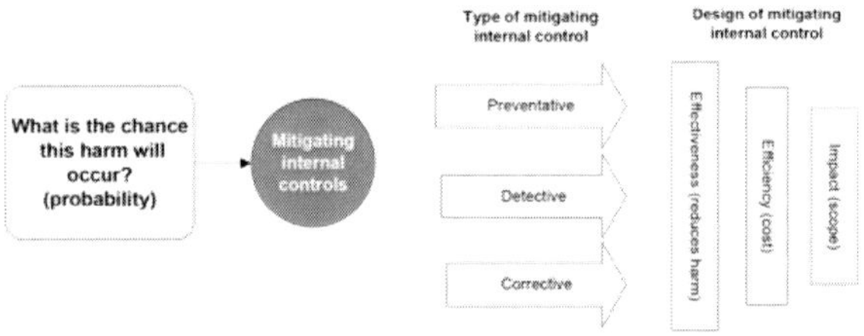

As a guide we have compiled the of tax controls every company should have in place over its provision process with the emphasis (as expected) on review as the key control.

As a guide we have compiled the list of tax controls every company should have in place over its provision process with the emphasis (as expected) on review as the key control.

- Ensure source information gathered from the accounting and other external departments is accurate.
    - Does your tax process ensure that raw data is referenced back to the trial balance or other supporting working papers to ensure there are no material differences?
- Ensure tax rates used for current and future tax calculations are correct.
    - Does your tax process ensure that rates used in calculations have been checked to an external source and are substantively enacted (depending on GAAP being used)?
- Ensure the accuracy of the tax calculations.
    - How does you tax department keep abreast of any changes in domestic and foreign tax legislation?
    - Does your tax process ensure that calculations are correct by re-calculating material numbers?
    - Does your department restrict access to spreadsheets and systems used for calculations?
    - Are changes made to spreadsheets and systems tracked and reviewed separately to ensure errors do not occur?

- Ensure that tax contingencies are adequately supported.
    - Does your tax process ensure that every contingency item is supported with a dollar amount, a related taxation year and the rationale for the contingency?
- Ensure the book to actual adjustment has been made.
    - Does your tax process ensure that two separate adjustments are recorded (i) prior year's tax provision estimate to tax return filed adjustment and (ii) prior year's tax return filed to the assessed amount?
    - Furthermore have you considered why there are significant differences (if any) and can the provision process be improved to reduce these adjustments.
- Ensure inputs for deferred tax balances are accurate and reasonable.
    - The decision of whether and where (short or long term) to record a deferred tax asset/liability may be partially based on the company's revenue forecast in specific jurisdictions, financing plans, planned acquisitions and divestitures, etc. Does your tax process ensure that tax is involved in these strategic discussions and has the most current information?

- Ensure that tax entries are properly authorized and posted correctly to general ledger and tax accounts.
    - This has two parts as payments into and adjustments between tax accounts (taxing authority accounts) should be properly authorized and reconciled on a monthly basis to ensure balances correct for each legal entity and taxation year.
    - The second part is to ensure that the journal entries made to record the payments, adjustments, accruals, and expense, etc are properly authorized and the general ledger accounts reconcile to tax working papers.
- Ensure that the income tax balances are recorded according to generally accepted accounting principles.
    - Does your tax process ensure there is adequate documentation to support that taxes are recorded correctly?
    - How does the tax department keep abreast of changes to accounting for its domestic and foreign companies?
    - Have accounting tax policies been approved by the chief financial officer and agreed to by external auditors?

- Ensure that all tax-related figures used for public dissemination have been agreed.
    - Does your tax process ensure the tax department reviews and agrees with all other tax-related figures in the MD&A, annual report and annual information return?
- Ensure that a Tax Plan Implementation Review is performed.
    - Does your tax process ensure that tax plans implemented have been appropriately authorized, implemented and are regularly measured to ensure they are achieving planning goals?

The Most Important Piece

We generally see two streams of personnel in tax departments - those with company or industry knowledge and less tax technical knowledge or those parachuted in with technical savvy and less business knowledge. It takes a while for the two to merge and it is sometimes difficult to move the staff in the direction you want.

One of the most significant tax risks are the gaps in knowledge and experience in the staff. Only once you can objectively see these holes can you start to fill them in. The natural outflow is an employee development plan - lifelong learning and empowerment, focused on being part of the company's growth. These are the basis for their goals for performance measurement.

We do however admit that tax can be a difficult area in which to set performance measurement standards for employees. Some potential tax goals and measurement methods are:

- Level appropriate tax planning ideas or handling a smaller piece of an overall plan successfully;
- Reducing tax audit adjustments;
- Developing or leading cross training of other staff;
- Completion of compliance requirements on a timely basis;
- Minimising penalty and interest on compliance;
- Initiating tax-related projects outside the department – assisting in product development process or business development areas; and
- Undertaking process improvement within the department.

It is important that each employee feel empowered and by empowerment I mean each employee should be permitted the authority (and associated risk) to make decisions based on their experience and knowledge (feeding straight back into the tax risk framework.)

Filling in the gaps sounds easier than it is, but there is very little directed education out there for tax. Our approach is to start with sharing the knowledge. We have a process to create job descriptions based on processes staff handles each day. From those job descriptions, procedure manuals be established which can help support cross training and push the knowledge down to more junior staff. There are already some great tax technical courses available but we found few addressed the more routine administrative issues and have designed guides around our tools to support these gaps. The other hole we fill is hands-on training – we have experienced tax personnel (not "trainers") that come in and provide in-house training on your issues using your systems. Each session is customised to address the gaps your staff currently have making it effective and efficient. You may be able to find something similar with your local professional accounting firm.

And Finally - the Sales Pitch

Our goal is for clients to feel confident they have captured virtually all tax risk and have effective, efficient key controls in place in order to monitor and report appropriately. We know with a little help and some tools, companies can do it themselves.

Why a More Tailored Approach Is Better

The Big Four have developed their own in-house tax risk methodologies; they have a team that deals with assessing an organization's risks and how to best mitigate those risks. We know firsthand, we worked at one of them. All of the Big Four claim to have a distinct philosophy, which can be very rigid but in reality they are all fairly similar in thought. We have the same thoughts and our own approach but we want to be part of your team and not a separate team.

Most companies have a pretty good idea of how they want to see information structured and reported. We try and work with our clients – they already know what works for them. If a client does not like the presentation of our tool kit's look, we can modify it to look however the client wants – we are flexible.

The Tax Governance Path

We guide you through the best practices of tax risk governance in order to complete your tax risk strategy framework. We help you align tax risk to the overall corporate vision. We will help write board level and senior management mandates or you can use our stand-alone templates. The wording is contiguous between your mandates all the way down to your policies.

We will also create your initial board reporting package. The audit committee is responsible for ensuring that the enterprise risk-management systems are working in the finance area and doesn't tend to get standardized packages in the respect of tax. Just because people are on the audit committee does not necessarily mean that they can identify the company's tax risk themselves.

We help clients hone the wording in their packages and fine tune the amount of information that they provide, we even address the way it is presented. We help craft it so the board gets information it understands; it assures them the risk management policies are being adhered to and can understand what is going on in the tax department.

The Tax Compliance Guide

When you step into the compliance risk area, you have, obviously, risk of noncompliance, risk of penalties and interests, and risk of audit adjustments due to an error in filing. One of the things that we like to do is sit down with the company, and, through an interview process develop a schedule which lists every tax filing that needs to be prepared, by whom, in what jurisdiction, and by what time.

To help with this, we developed a tool to upload the individual tasks into your on-line calendar – everyone gets assigned their specific tasks. You identify the risks by actually going through all of your entities, where they actually operate, and what has to be filed. You can assess the risk because now you know what the penalties and interests might be if you do not file. You also have a great way to assign the responsibilities and monitor to make sure it is actually getting done.

Tax risk can expand beyond just your normal income tax. There is also value-added tax, there are information returns, and there are regulatory and banking tax-related filings that have to occur. All of these can get tracked and monitored.

Companies with slip filings, T5, T5018, and NR4s sent out annually can minimize manual errors and ease the review process. We have built tool kits that are built in spreadsheet based to upload directly into tax preparation software.

The Tax Accounting Coordinates

A large area is the tax risk embedded in financial statements and related items. Most people hone in on this area because of the chaos of getting numbers on your financial statements each quarter, or each year-end. That is what people focus on for internal control testing, and your external auditors will focus on it because it is going in your audited financials and annual report.

One of the ways to ensure that the risk on this has actually been identified is that we walk it through with you, setting up and building a tax provision template, integrated right into your GL if required, that underpins your financial statements. It gives your auditors great comfort because all of those numbers are built, tested, and developed to support the numbers on your financial statements.

We can link your financial statement numbers off your provisions directly into a template built for tax disclosure notes. There is also ancillary support that occurs around your accounting numbers. Those are things like:

- Supporting documentation for recording tax benefits.
- A worksheet to track all of your tax status by year and jurisdiction; which years under audit, which years have waivers attached to them.
- A tax internal control matrix for CFO certification.

The Tax Resource Roadmap

Your CPL Tax Resource Road Map is a way to objectively review people's processes and the inherent compensation plans related to the tax department. Our tool kits, interviews and checklists tease out the known and unknown gaps in knowledge and experience among the staff. We help managers create plans to develop their people into better resources, and link these development plans to a performance measurement matrix.

You need to create your performance measurement in order to link what the tax department values and establish the behaviors that will enforce that value to a plan so you can measure it.

We have a short and sweet methodology where we help create job descriptions. From these job descriptions and process descriptions, we write procedure manuals. Because of the extensive nature of this work, we do in house training geared towards specific gaps and knowledge, and offer online webinars for more basic tax training.

More??

Please go to our website for more information www.theclaretpartners.com or send an email to info@theclaretpartners.com with your questions.

Further Reading and Research:

Centre for Tax Policy and Administration (OECD) has a great paper on this subject (GAP003).

Here's How to Manage Your Tax Risk like a Big Company without the Big Expense

You already know there will always be risks to manage. But have you considered there may be risks you are not currently addressing?

That is where we come in. We help CFOs just like you systematize your tax risk within your ERM so that you can capture all the risks.

Step 1: We work with you to identify your existing tax risk needs and design a customized integration workflow specific to your business and industry.

Step 2: We help you train your team to apply the new templates and ensure everyone is on board with their role.

Step 3: We provide customized supplemental training as needed for ongoing support and training.

Most CFOs think that it takes outsourcing their risk management to one of the Big Four to effectively manage their risk.

Now you can manage your tax risk like a Big Company without the big expense by keeping the work in house with the people who know your business inside and out.

If you would like us to help, just send an email to: info@theclaretpartners.com and we will take it from there.